To _____

From _____

THE BOOK OF VALENTINES

Sonnie O'Reilly

Fontana
An Imprint of HarperCollinsPublishers

Fontana
An Imprint of HarperCollins*Publishers*,
77–85 Fulham Palace Road,
Hammersmith, London W6 8JB

Published by Fontana 1991

9 8 7 6 5 4 3 2 1

First published in Great Britain by
Angus & Robertson (UK) Ltd 1991

Text copyright © Sonnie O'Reilly 1983, 1991

The Author asserts the moral right to
be identified as the author of this work

A catalogue record for this book is
available from the British Library

ISBN 0 00 637823 4

Set in Souvenir

Printed in Great Britain by
Scotprint Ltd, Musselburgh

All rights reserved. No part of this publication may be
reproduced, stored in a retrieval system, or transmitted,
in any form or by any means, electronic, mechanical,
photocopying, recording or otherwise, without the prior
permission of the publishers.

This book is sold subject to the condition that it shall not,
by way of trade or otherwise, be lent, re-sold, hired out or
otherwise circulated without the publisher's prior consent
in any form of binding or cover other than that in which it
is published and without a similar condition including this
condition being imposed on the subsequent purchaser.

ACKNOWLEDGEMENTS

The author acknowledges the voluntary contributions of a number of special friends whose efforts have enriched this work and thereby made it an even more comprehensive collection. I speak of Helen Desmond, Martin Ruane, Ann Muckley, Declan Savage, Mary Ruane and Joan Hayes.

The work will never become the *Book of Kells* of the twentieth century, but nevertheless stands a good chance, in the not too distance future, of becoming a beloved and cherished 'reference book' of all that is good, cheerful and harmless.

For all my lifetime I have been collecting these valentines which in days gone by were usually written in autograph books. In so far as I am aware they are all traditional and if I have, through error, used someone's material I beg their forgiveness.

> When I am dead and in my grave
> And all my bones are rotten,
> This little book will tell my name,
> When I am long forgotten.

Sonnie O'Reilly

To my wife Nora

You're so lovable
You're so sweet
To be your valentine
Would make my day complete

Dear Valentine
Your eyes are blue
Your heart is true
Your lips divine
When they meet mine

Kiss under a lily
Kiss under a rose
But the best place to kiss
Is under the nose

A bunch of roses
A glass of wine
I'm asking you
Will you be mine?

Roses are red
Violets are blue
In my life
There's a place for you

If a snowflake was a kiss
I'd send you a blizzard

I like your lips
I like your style
But most of all
I like your smile

Tu-lips in the garden
Tu-lips in the park
But the tu-lips I like best
Are your tu-lips in the dark

A ring is round
And has no end
That's how long
I'll be your friend

When the Golden Sun is sinking
And your mind from care is free
When you are thinking of your friends
Won't you sometimes think of me?

I wish you were a china cup
From which I drink my tea
And every time I take a cup
I get a kiss from thee

May you sail on the sea of ambition
And land on the shore of success

Thou shall not covet thy neighbour's goods
Not even a penny bun
But say thanks to the Lord
He did not forbid thee
To court thy neighbour's son

They walked the lane together
The night was full of stars
They reached the gate together
He opened for her the bars
She neither smiled or thanked him
For indeed she knew not how
For he was only a farmer's son
And she a Kerry cow

Friendship is a golden cord
Which links two hearts together
If you don't break this golden cord
We'll be friends forever and ever

Two in a hammock
Attempted to kiss
But all of a sudden
They turned up like SIHL

You want triplets
I want twins
Let's get married
And see who wins

There are silver ships
There are gold ships
But there are no ships
Like friendships

Flowers may wither
Leaves may die
Friends may forget you
But never will I

Always remember
And never forget
The nicest person
You ever met

Roses are red
Violets are blue
Sugar is sweet
And so are you

I thought of you the other day
Because you were so far away
Some day soon you will be mine
_____ my sweet Valentine

From me to you
With love and kisses
How I'd love to be your Mrs

God made trees
Man made fences
God made the boys
To kiss pretty wenches

I wish I were a cigarette
Wrapped up nice and neat
Then every little pull you take
Both our lips would meet

I bet you a cuddle
I bet you a kiss
I bet you'll never guess
Who sent you this

It happened when I saw your smile
Your eyes looked into mine
I loved you dearly since that day
Be my valentine

A little note short and true
Just to say 'I love you'

Of all the mermaids
In the sea
You're the only
One for me

I am putting pen to paper
To a love that's so divine
And all I want to know is
Will you be my valentine?

Meeting is a pleasure
Parting is a pain
God be with you _____
Until we meet again

Holy Father full of grace
Bless _____ happy face
Bless his hair that tends to curl
Keep him away from other girls
Bless his hands that are so strong
Tell him to keep them where they belong
Bless his eyes that are so sweet
Tell him they knock me off my feet
But above all this keep us together
Not for now, but for now and ever

If beauty was a rock
You'd be a mountain
If good looks were a drop
You'd be an ocean

Under the bramble bush
Under the tree
_____ kissed _____
While sitting on his knee

As sure as the Devil
Has a tail
My love for you
Will never fail

Oranges grow in Japan
Peaches grow there too
But it takes a place like _____
To grow a peach like you

They say that kisses are the food of life –
Well then I'm very, very hungry

Two in a car
Two little kisses
Two weeks later
Mr and Mrs

A kiss is but a simple thing
And yet a kiss is sweet
But when given by the one you love
It's considered as a treat

If this sender you can name
All these kisses you can claim

When you are old and weary
And my face you cannot see
Remember it was _____
Who wrote these lines to thee

I must not say I love you
You're someone else's boy
I must not long to hold you
That's someone else's joy
My eyes light up
When someone says your name
You're someone else's love
But I want you all the same

To someone who is so enchanting
A real live dream come true
I send my love with all my heart
To my wonderful darling you

You're a wonder
You're worthwhile
I'll tell you something
You're my style

Roses are red
Violets are blue
Tender regards
From you know who

American boys are beautiful
English boys are smart
But it takes a boy from _____
To steal away a heart

A kiss on paper
Is not so sweet
But we'll improve
Next time we meet

Remember M Remember E
Put them together and remember ME

When the church bells are ringing
And calling you to pray
Will you sometimes think about me
When I'm miles and miles away

A house is made of bricks and stone
But a home is made of love alone

When making new friends
Forget not the old
The new ones are silver
But the old ones are gold

My heart to you I'll give
If you give yours to me
We'll lock them both together
And throw away the key

Kisses spread disease it's stated
Kiss me quick I'm vaccinated

I wish you were an old shoe
And me a piece of leather
For some old cobbler to come along
And stick us both together

If	As	No	Our
you	I	knife	love
love	love	can	in
me	you	cut	two

Kisses are sweet when two lips meet
But very cold on paper!

Why do I love you _____?
There are so many reasons it's true
But I know the most important one
It's just because you're you

I don't know how it happened
I only know it's true
That there's a place in my heart
No one can fill but you

I walked across the dance floor
I really took my time
I didn't want to run and fall
In reaching my valentine

Look under the moon
Look under the lamp
If you want to know my name
Look under the stamp

Up the ladder 1, 2, 3
If you fall, fall for me

The higher the mountain
The cooler the breeze
The younger the couple
The tighter the squeeze

If love was against the law
And a kiss was a crime
The person reading this
Would now be serving time

I wish I was a big blue duck egg
A bonnie blue-eyed smasher
And you beside me in the pan
A long, long streaky rasher

Dear Valentine
I feel so blue
Why am I always
Thinking of you?

A mountain is high
A lake is deep
My love for you
Will always keep

My pen is bad
My ink is pale
But my love for you
Will never fail

To kiss a miss is awfully simple
But to miss a kiss is simply awful

My darling little ducky
I love you clean and mucky
Come into my arms you bundle of charms
And stick to my heart like putty

I pass you every day in the street
But somehow we never seem to meet
I look at you, I smile and try
To catch a wink from your big blue eyes

If I'm in heaven and you're not there
I'll carve your name on the golden chair
For all the angels there to see
I love you and you love me
And if you're not there by judgement day
I'll know you've gone the other way
So just to prove my love is true
I'll go to hell just to be with you

Your eyes are blue
Your heart is true
Your lips are divine
When they meet mine

Happy dreams
Sweet repose
Think of me
When you're under the clothes

Think of me always
Think of me true
For you know _____
I always loved you

Roses are red
Lavender blue
If you'll have me
I'll have you

My heart is like a head of cabbage
It's really split in two
The leaves I'd give to others
But the heart I'd keep for you

I pray the years be good to us
And all our hopes fulfil
That every day that passes by
Shall find us closer still

True hearted, whole hearted
Faithful ever be
And if you really wish it
Your friend I'll always be

This is my verse
It's simple and true
Dear _____
I love you

You are 2 Good
         2 Be
         ———
         4 Gotten

I was sitting in my room
I was looking at the time
And all the time I was sitting there
My thoughts were on you dear Valentine

It's true I wish you health and plenty
It's true I wish you wealth
But what I wish you most of all
Is what you wish yourself

Our love is young
Our hearts entwined
You and me dear Valentine

Ever since Dear _____
I first set eyes on you
I fell for you completely
Couldn't you say you love me too

Two and two are four
Five and four are nine
I'm asking you dear _____
Will you be my Valentine?

I swear by all the stars above
It's you dear _____ I'll always love

I'd climb the highest mountain
Or swim the ocean blue
I'd battle through the fiercest storm
Dear _____ for you

Though seas may roll between
And many miles divide
Our thoughts dear in a moment
Can cross the ocean wide
Just listen to the message
In sending through the blue
Come closer, dear and whisper
Lest the world hears, 'I love you'

There's a little blue flower
And in the centre a white white spot
It grows in the sunny bower
And they call it the forget-me-not
You are the little blue flower
Your heart is the white, white spot
Your smiles are the sunny bower
So darling, forget me not

Remembrance is as sweet as ever
The old wish just as new
Time cannot change nor distance sever
The links of friendship true

Bright be the future that lieth before thee
Loving and loved may you go on your way
May God in his kindness watch tenderly o'er you
Guarding and guiding you by night and by day

She stood at the altar so pretty and fair
She stood by the altar her heart was not there
She stood by the altar and wasn't it shocking
She suddenly thought of the hole in her stocking

Worry not over the future
The present is all thou hast
The future will soon be the present
And the present will soon be the past

In the shadows of the night
In the sky pale dawn
When the sun is high and bright
When its rays are homeward drawn
Every moment sad and gay
All the long day true
Thoughts of mine forever stray
Back again to you

Give me a thought in the hour of pleasure
Remember in the hour of leisure
And if I forgot in the hour of care
Remember me in the hour of prayer

Remember me in friendship
Remember me at heart
Remember me dear _____
When you and I doth part
Remember me and don't forget
Remember me forever
For many the happy hours we spent
In _____ together

These few words are tendered
By a friend sincere and true
Hoping to be remembered
When far away from you

As I sit beside the cottage
And gaze across the sea
My thoughts fly wandering backwards
To a land that used to be
I think of one who loved me
Who was ever by my side
And I wonder if she thinks of me
Across the rolling tide

Thousands of miles may divide us
Oceans may keep us apart
But the day I was with you in _____
Will always be dear to my heart

There are many words when spoken
A meaning deep convey
There are many words though simple
We find difficult to say
There are many words that cause a tear
To dim the loving eye
But I think that saddest word of all
Is the simplest word 'goodbye'

From memory's page
Time cannot plot
Three little words
Forget-me-not

I wish you health I wish you wealth
I wish you gold in store
I wish you heaven after death
What could I wish you more

I wish you luck I wish you joy
I wish you first a little boy
And when his hair begins to curl
I wish you then a little girl

Some day I will look back with pleasure
On the battles we fought, lose or win
Still there will be one little treasure
I'll keep with me unto the end

There's a wee vacant spot in my memory
That I keep for friends who are true
But now all these memories have vanished
And that spot has been conquered by you

When you are married
And the twins on your knee
For the sake of old acquaintance
Call one after me

Remember me when this you see
I ask for nothing more
For we may never meet again
When holidays are o'er

May happiness surround you
Like the sweet scent of flowers
And Mercy shed her golden wings
To bring you sleeping hours

The clouds may rest on the present
And sorrows on the days that are gone
But no night is so utterly cheerless
That we may not look for a dawn

There is a little word
To some it's very dear
In English it's forget-me-not
In French it's *souvenir*

'Tis hard to lose the boy you love
When your heart is so full of hope
But it's harder still to find the towel
When your eyes are full of soap

I do not write for glory
I do not write for fame
I write to be remembered
And so I write my name

Two is company
Three is a crowd
Four in a bed
Is not allowed

There are many miles between us
And distance be our lot
But the flower that grows between us
Is the sweet forget-me-not

What shall I write?
What shall it be?
Two little words
Remember me

Love it is an awful thing
It makes a man a fool
It takes away his appetite
And wears away his shoes

Remember me when this you see
And do not me forget
Although we're only flirting now
On you my heart is set

Love it is a killing thing
Did you ever feel the pain?
I'd rather for to be in jail
Than to be in love again

Long may you live
Happy be your life
Blessed be the little man
That takes you as his wife

Dearest dear my heart's delight
Of you I'm dreaming every night
And in my dreams I plainly see
That you were meant to sleep with me
The ring is round and has no end
To marry you I do intend
So let us hope that we shall meet
Between the blanket and the sheet

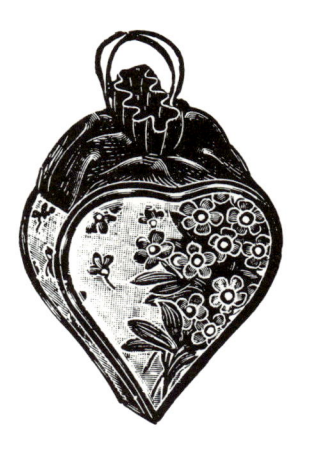

This is the dove that flew above
And seldom lost a feather
And if I don't marry the boy that I love
I'll live alone forever

Perhaps this won't mean much to you
When you are feeling blue
But I hope you will remember me
A fellow student true

When days are dark and friends are few
Remember me as I do you
It only takes a little spot
To write the words forget-me-not

A smile is quite a funny thing
It wrinkles up your face
And when it's gone you'll never find
Its sweet hiding place
But far more wonderful than this
To see what smiles can do
You smile at one he smiles on you
And so one smile makes two

When the beaming sun is shining
And you sit down to tea
Just pause and think before you drink
Of _____ and of me

Many a ship was lost at sea
For want of war and rudder
Many a boy has lost his girl
For walking with another

The world is wide, the sea is deep
A young man's heart is hard to keep

Never let your chances
Like the sunbeams pass you by
For you never miss the water
Till the well runs dry

Remember me at the washing tub
Remember me at every rub
And if the water be ever so hot
Lather away and forget me not

Remember me on the river
Remember me on the lake
Remember me on your wedding day
And send me a slice of cake

'Tis you I love and shall forever
You may always but I will never
And if separation be our lot
Then dearest dear forget me not

If you were a post card
And I the stamp could be
I'd lick you till I'm sure you stick
Through thick and thin to me

Though rocks and seas divide us
And your face I cannot see
You may think you are forgotten
But this shall never be

In the parlour there were three
She, the parlour lamp, and he
Two is company, three is a crowd
And so the parlour lamp went out

When sitting on a lonely spot
Awaiting a lover to see
Turn your heart towards _____
And kindly think of me

Remember me when this you see
And bear me in your mind
And don't be like the weather cock
That changes with the wind
But just be like the turtle dove
That sits in yonder tree
Waiting for her own true love
As I may wait for thee

Our love is pure and simple
I'm pure and you're simple

I kissed a boy from _____
I kissed him as a token
I broke the main spring of his heart
And left his mouth wide open

You think you are a hard guy
The way you shout and pose
But every time I look at you
Your finger's up your nose

You look like Clark Gable
Your eyes are like his too
But when it comes to kissing
You taste of Irish stew

Roses are red
Violets are blue
The tap in the kitchen
Reminds me of you –
Drip, Drip, Drip

When I sealed this valentine
My heart began to thump
My hand began to shake
And in my throat there was a lump
You may think I was thinking of you
But no I'm allergic to envelope glue

I love you, I love you, I love you, I do
But don't get excited, I love monkeys too

My dearest darling ducky
Behind your ears are mucky
But never mind, love is blind
My dearest darling ducky

God made the Scottish
God made the Dutch
But when God made you
He didn't make much

When God was giving out good looks
There was a long, long queue
I was in the middle
But where the hell were you?

Roses are red
Violets are blue
Your mother is good looking
What happened to you?

Roses are red
Cabbage is green
My face is funny
But yours is a scream

They say it is a sin to love
I really don't know why
But if you sin in loving a boy
You're sinning all your life